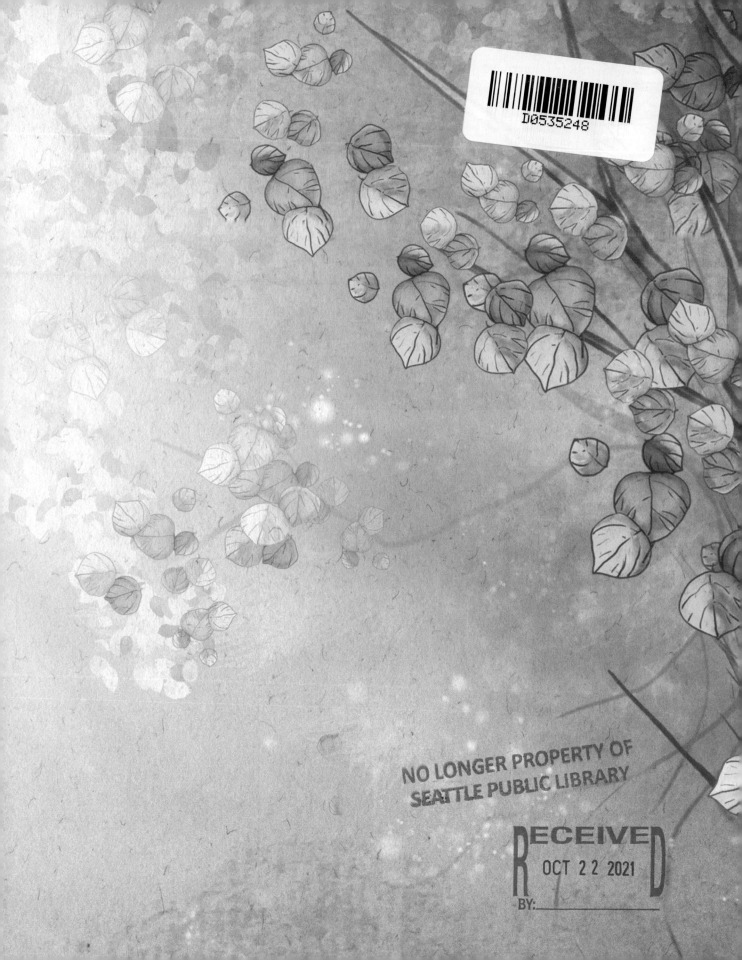

PANDO

A Living Wonder of Trees

BY KATE ALLEN FOX

ILLUSTRATED BY TURINE TRAN

CAPSTONE EDITIONS

a capstone imprint

Published by Capstone Editions,
an imprint of Capstone.
1710 Roe Crest Drive
North Mankato, Minnesota 56003
capstonepub.com

Library of Congress Cataloging-in-Publication Data
is available on the Library of Congress website.

ISBN: 9781684462773 (hardcover)
ISBN: 9781684463855 (ebook PDF)

Summary: *Pando* is an inspiring tribute to a grove of quaking aspen trees connected by their roots to form one of the world's oldest and largest living things. Author Kate Allen Fox engages readers' senses to help convey the challenges Pando faces and share how we all can be part of the solution.

Image Credits: Shutterstock: Brett Taylor Photography, 29, (bottom), IRINA OKSENOYD, design element, throughout, Kreig Rasmussen, 28, (top), pandapaw, design element, Cover, Reuben Jolley Photography, 29, (top), Wikimedia: USDA/J Zapell, 28, (bottom)

Designed by Tracy Davies

Printed and bound in China. 4206

For my sprouts, Calvin and Charlie —KAF

Near a humming highway,
a giant forest stands firm.

Thousands of trees—almost exactly
alike—whisper in the wind,

stretching higher than you can climb,

farther than you can see.

All these trees tremble
in the same breeze.

Their yellow leaves shimmer
in the same sunshine,

dancing to the same symphony
of chirping birds.

At least for now. . . .

The Trembling Giant is an aspen grove
(*Populus tremuloides)* in Utah.

For now, there are more trees

than stars you can see on a clear night
than species of fish in the sea
than miles that stretch around the world.

All these trees seem to stand apart.

But . . . under the inky soil,
their roots link—

tree,
hooked to tree,
hooked to tree.

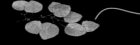

- You can see about 2,000 stars on a clear night.
- There about 32,000 known species of fish alive today.
- Earth is about 24,901 miles around at the equator.

All these trees are one being, called by one name:

Pando.

In the old language of Latin, its name means *I spread.*

And spread Pando has.

All the trees in Pando look similar, taste the same to animals, and change colors together in the fall.

Pando began life as a seed.

He was
smaller than you,
smaller than a mouse,
smaller even than an acorn or a pea.

He was a seed no larger than
a single speck of pepper.

Aspens can be male or female. Pando is a male
and is often called "he."

This tiny seed grew into a tree.

The tree's roots wriggled under the earth,
searching for an open spot,
and climbed back up until . . .

POP!

Another tree sprouted.

It grew, and grew, and grew . . .

When Pando's roots come out of the ground to make a new tree, it is called cloning. New aspens can grow through cloning or with seeds, but cloning is much more common.

The sprouts kept sprouting
for years and years and years.

The sprouts grew . . .

as roads closed in,
as houses popped up,
as the roar of engines replaced gentle footsteps.

Today Pando is
made up of 47,000 trees—

one of the biggest
living things in the world.

Most aspen clones cover between 1 and 20 acres.
Pando is the biggest and the oldest. He weighs more
than 13 million pounds and covers 106 acres—
more than 100 football fields.

Some scientists say he started growing
as far back as 12,000 years ago. . . .

15,000 years ago	humans first came to North America
12,000 years ago	end of last Ice Age; Pando first sprouted
5,500 years ago	invention of the wheel
4,600 years ago	the Great Pyramids were built
2,000 years ago	chess was first played
50 years ago	scientists began studying Pando

But Pando isn't getting bigger anymore.

Humans have changed his home.

He's shrinking . . .

as his new trees are chewed up by animals,
as new places to sprout become scarce,
as new buildings block his mighty spread.

New trees must sprout for Pando to survive. These new trees are small and often get eaten by deer and other animals. As Pando's environment has changed, these tree-munching animals have increased, and other threats have also grown.

And Pando may keep shrinking.

His trees may vanish,

one
by one
by one,
until . . .

there are no trees to climb,
no branches to sway,
no leaves to quake.

He may shrink smaller than a speck of pepper
and disappear.

Unless . . .

Some forest fires can actually help the environment by killing off diseases and enriching the soil. But there are buildings near Pando, so fires are not allowed to burn.

We help Pando find what he needs—
good dirt and open space.

To the north and south, east and west,
from Alaska to Mexico, California to Maine,
other aspens spread their roots too,

all of them searching for room to grow.

Aspen clones can be found throughout North America, from southern Mexico to northern Alaska, including in many U.S. and Canadian national parks.

We can protect their homes
so they can survive and spread again.

And, as they spread,
they can make new homes
for beavers and bears, rabbits and wrens.

People are working to save Pando by building fences and
moving livestock to protect him from hungry animals. As
scientists learn more about how to protect Pando, they can
use what they learn to protect other trees too.

Like trees linked by their roots,
people, animals, and plants
are all connected.

We can make a world where we *all*
have room to grow.

In giant forests or favorite parks,
across the world or around the corner,

we can
protect the land,
care for the soil,
and keep the water clean.

Animals and plants—along with nonliving things like water, rocks, and dirt—are all parts of ecosystems. When one part of the ecosystem is threatened, it can affect every other part.

So for years to come . . .

trees everywhere can whisper in the wind,
shimmer in the sunshine,
dance to the birdsong,

and stretch

higher than you could climb,
farther than you could see.

PANDO

Pando is in Fishlake National Forest in Richfield, Utah.

Pando consists of about 47,000 quaking aspens. The trees were named for the way the leaves flutter in even the slightest breeze.

Like many deciduous trees (trees that lose their leaves), Pando's leaves are green in the summer and turn gold in the fall.

In 2006, Pando was named one of "40 Wonders of America" by the U.S. Postal Service and was honored with a stamp. People come from all over the world to see Pando.

GLOSSARY

An **aspen** is a kind of tree belonging to the poplar family. The quaking aspen is found in more areas of North America than any other tree. Other types of aspens are found in Europe, Africa, and Asia.

A **clone** is a copy of a living thing. Clones have the exact same DNA—genetic material—as the thing they were cloned from. This is different from other types of reproduction where parents and offspring only share some DNA.

An **ecosystem** is all the living and nonliving things in an area, including plants, animals, fungi, bacteria, water, rocks, and soil. Living creatures depend on other parts of their ecosystem to survive.

Roots are the part of a plant that is usually hidden underground. They help a plant stay in place and take in water and nutrients from the soil. Pando's roots also create new sprouts, allowing Pando to reproduce.

A **seed** is the part of a plant that can grow into a new plant. Seeds need the right conditions—usually water, sunshine, air, and soil—to grow. Pando started as a seed.

Soil is dirt where plants can grow. Soil is called "rich" if it has nutrients that help plants grow.

A **sprout** is a young shoot of a plant. A new sprout usually shoots—or comes up—out of the ground.

HOW YOU CAN HELP

One of the most important things you can do is visit your local parks and **share your love of nature with others**. Whenever you hike, make sure to follow trail markers. Feet can trample the tender sprouts of new plants.

At home, you can reduce, reuse, and recycle—especially paper products, which are made from trees—to help **conserve natural resources**. You can also turn out lights when you leave a room and use less water by turning off the faucet while you're brushing your teeth.

By **planting a tree** in your community, you can help your local ecosystem thrive. Be sure to talk to someone at a garden center to learn what types of trees grow in your area and how you can best care for them.

You can also **support organizations that are working to protect aspen trees**, such as the Western Aspen Alliance. You can host a class fundraiser or bake sale and donate money to groups protecting trees. You can also write letters to your local officials, such as the mayor or city council, voicing support for conservation efforts in your area.

BIBLIOGRAPHY

Grant, Michael C., "The Trembling Giant," *Discover*, October 1, 1993, discovermagazine.com/planet-earth/the-trembling-giant

Klein, JoAnna, "Pando, the Most Massive Organism on Earth, Is Shrinking," *The New York Times*, October 17, 2018, nytimes.com/2018/10/17/science/pando-aspens-utah.html

Nace, Trevor, "The World's Largest Organism, Pando, Is Dying," *Forbes*, October 18, 2018, forbes.com/sites/trevornace/2018/10/18/the-worlds-largest-organism-pando-is-dying

National Park Service, "Quaking Aspen," January 21, 2021, nps.gov/brca/learn/nature/quakingaspen.htm

ABOUT THE AUTHOR

Kate Allen Fox lives in southern California with her husband and two sons. After a career as a public health professional, she combined her passions for research and writing and began creating picture books about science and nature. Her work has appeared in several publications, including *The New York Times*. This is her first picture book.

ABOUT THE ILLUSTRATOR

Award-winning artist **Turine Tran** takes inspiration from children, friends, nature, and her happy childhood. Through nostalgic, dreamy images, Turine invites readers to a world where a tiny wildflower can become a fantastic wonder. Born and raised in Saigon, Vietnam, Turine began her art study in 2001. Her journey led her to Singapore, France, and Scotland, where she obtained a masters of art degree in illustration from the prestigious Edinburgh College of Art. She went on to earn a PhD in the field. Besides making books to delight children and adults alike, Turine teaches illustration and is learning to cook and garden. She lives in Saigon with her two dogs.